Pika Country
Climate Change at the Top of the World

DOROTHY HINSHAW PATENT & MARLO GARNSWORTHY
Photographs by **DAN HARTMAN**

It's a chilly July morning at 10,000 feet on a mountain near Yellowstone National Park. The sun shines brightly on the colorful wildflowers dotting the grassy landscape.

All is silent until a squeaky bark rings out from a mound of jagged boulders.

Across the rock pile, a furry creature just smaller than a guinea pig stretches its neck and lets out a sharp answering squeak.

"I hear you, and this rock is *my* rock. Stay away!" it seems to say.

These hardy little creatures are called pikas, or rock rabbits. They look like they might be relatives of rats and mice, but they are actually related to rabbits.

The two pikas go their separate ways, scurrying through grass and flowers, gathering bundles of food between their teeth. They disappear among the rocks, returning with empty mouths.

All across the rock pile, it's scurry, scurry, hurry, hurry, gather as much as possible before the day warms up. Then the pikas scamper down through the cool, shady cracks between boulders and rocks to escape the heat of day.

Pikas need cool temperatures to gather food. They have a naturally high body temperature, so all this constant work makes them easily overheat on warm days.

In the early morning and evening, they come out from under the boulders.

The little rock rabbit snips grasses, flowers, and other plants and adds them to a **haypile** under an overhanging rock to dry.

Collecting enough food to last through the long, cold winter takes a lot of work.

Pikas are specially adapted to life in the chilly **alpine** environment among the rocks and plants.

In fact, pikas are usually only found in the mountains where the temperatures are cool. In temperatures warmer than 77 degrees Fahrenheit (25 degrees Celsius), pikas quickly overheat and die.

Pikas are truly stuck living up high.

Pikas are a perfect example of how **climate change** can endanger alpine animals.

Climate change refers to weather changes that are happening all around the world. Climate change causes warmer days, which can shorten the time it is cool enough each day for pikas to harvest plants for their winter stockpile. If their daily harvesting time decreases, they may not be able to gather enough food to last through the long winter.

The pikas in this book are American pikas. They can be found in the areas marked in brown on this map. Some other kinds of pikas live in different parts of Asia.

Unlike animals that **hibernate**, pikas stay awake during winter. Far under the snow, in the dark world among the rocks, they go about their lives.

When the weather allows, the pikas come up to the surface to **forage** for food near their rock pile. But they mostly rely on the haypiles they collected over the summer to survive.

In addition to their stockpile of food, pikas need a deep layer of snow above to **insulate** them from the extreme winter cold in the mountains. Otherwise, they could freeze to death.

But as alpine areas warm, there is less snowpack to protect pikas during winter.

As climate change warms their **habitat**, pikas have no choice but to move farther up the mountain to where it is cooler.

But there's a limit to up.

Today, scientists are worried about the effects of climate change on pikas and other high mountain life.

MOUNTAIN GOATS

A WEASEL
HUNTING A PIKA

RED FOX

A PINE MARTEN
EATING A PIKA

Everything is connected in the natural world. Changes for one **species** can lead to changes for other living things.

Pikas are one of the most important sources of food for **predators** such as weasels, foxes, and pine martens that share their alpine habitat. If pikas become scarce or disappear, these predators will have a harder time finding enough to eat.

WEASEL

FERRUGINOUS HAWK

PRAIRIE FALCON

GOLDEN EAGLE

As well as affecting local animals, climate change affects animals that are traveling through the mountains.

Raptors, such as eagles, from farther north **migrate** south over the Rocky Mountains in the fall. But by that time, all the **prey** animals except pikas may already be hibernating. That means pikas are their only available food as the raptors fly through the high mountain passes.

As pika populations decline, the effect on migrating birds can be devastating.

PIKA FOOD WEB

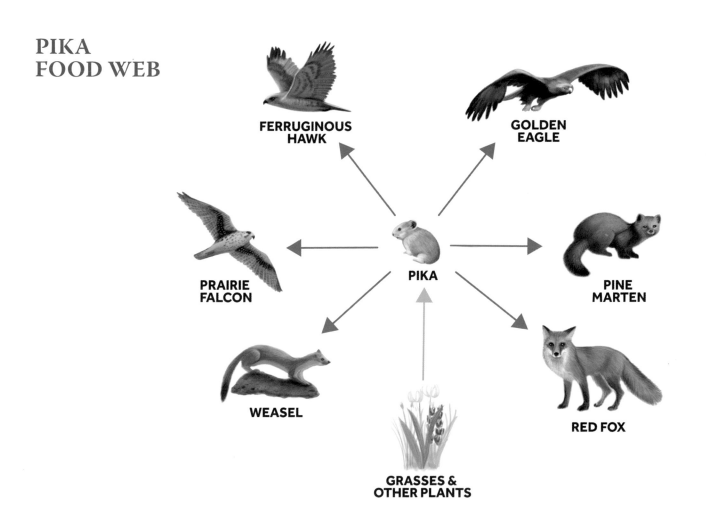

It is not only pikas and their predators that are in trouble. The changing climate creates problems for alpine plants, too.

In spring, alpine meadows are ablaze with colorful wildflowers. But climate change is causing some to flower earlier, often before insect **pollinators** have woken from their winter hibernation. Without pollination, plants cannot produce seeds.

BUMBLEBEE

SULPHUR BUTTERFLY

Even if they are pollinated, early-blooming flowers may still be at risk from a late frost. An unexpected cold spell might cause them to die before they produce seeds.

FLOWER FLY

Trees are affected by climate change, too. Warmer winters and **droughts** have allowed insects called pine bark beetles to survive at higher **elevations** than in the past. They attack whitebark pine trees and quickly kill them.

PINE BARK BEETLE

DYING WHITEBARK PINES

BLACK
BEAR

RED SQUIRREL

CLARK'S NUTCRACKER

Whitebark pines produce pine nuts, and bears use this rich food to fatten them up for hibernation. Nutcrackers and squirrels stash away these nuts for the winter. When the pines die, there is less food for these animals.

GLACIER LILY

GOLDEN-MANTLED GROUND SQUIRREL

RASPBERRY PLANT

If climate change continues, plant and tree populations will continue to decline, leaving pikas and other plant-eating animals hungry.

ALPINE FOOD WEB

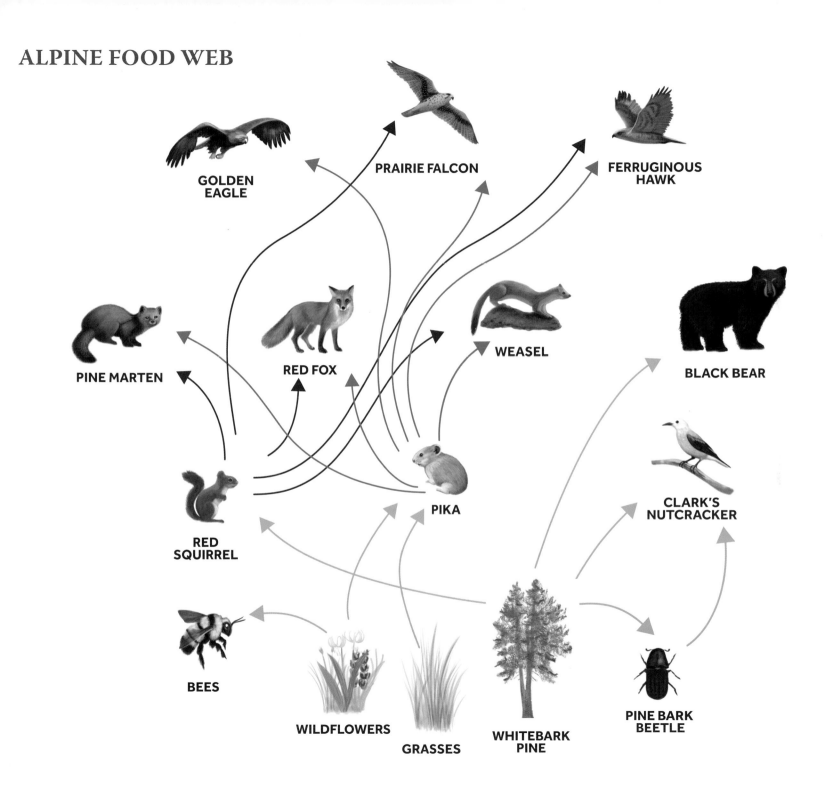

ROSY-FINCH

YELLOW-BELLIED
MARMOT

GRIZZLY BEAR

Like the pikas, many alpine plants and animals have begun to move higher to escape the effects of climate change. But as pikas and other alpine organisms move upward, the space for them lessens and their numbers decrease. Species that are forced to move higher up to survive may find themselves competing for **resources** with species that already live there. If this process continues, the living things that need cool, moist weather will have no place to go.

MOUNTAIN FOX

**LIVABLE HABITAT
IN THE PAST**

**LIVABLE HABITAT
NOW**

As pika populations decline, their survival as a species is increasingly at risk. Fewer individuals means fewer opportunities for **breeding**. It also means that a local pika population might not survive a disaster, such as an especially harsh season.

People enjoy warmth and sunshine, but for plants and animals that depend on cold weather and enough snow, warmer, drier weather causes hardship and population decline.

The future of pikas and other alpine species depends on the future of our planet's climate.

Fortunately, there are things people can do to help remedy climate change. Together we can work for a cleaner, cooler world in which all of our planet's species—from pikas to humans—can thrive.

WHAT IS CLIMATE CHANGE?

Climate change is the change in our planet's average temperature, winds, **precipitation**, and other conditions. Today, from their studies of the planet's history, scientists believe the climate is warming faster than at any time before.

The main cause of climate change is our burning of **fossil fuels**. Each time we burn the gas and coal that power our factories, fuel our cars, heat our homes, and keep our lights on, gases such as **carbon dioxide** are released. These gases are called **greenhouse gases**. Greenhouse gases act like a blanket around the planet. They stop heat from the sun from escaping back out to space. This is causing our planet to get warmer.

This warming is not only heating the planet and making life tough for cold-loving species; it is also creating more extreme weather events, such as stronger hurricanes, floods, and even extreme cold and blizzards. It is causing severe droughts and devastating forest fires in places like California and Australia. It is melting the ice in alpine and polar regions. As the Antarctic and Greenland Ice Sheets and mountain glaciers worldwide melt, they are raising sea level around the world. This is already affecting island and coastal communities, and it is expected to get worse as warming continues.

In addition to our cars and homes and factories, air travel is also a huge source of greenhouse gas emissions. And the cows we keep for meat and dairy products, such as milk and cheese, are a large source of **methane**, another greenhouse gas. It's hard to believe, but cows, which burp and fart methane as they digest their food, make a big contribution to greenhouse gases around the world. Cows and other livestock contribute around 15% of greenhouse gas emissions worldwide.

When the human population was smaller, this wasn't a problem, but there are now a lot more people on Earth than there used to be. That means we are burning more fossil fuels and raising more cattle than ever before. And the human population is currently growing by more than 80 million people per year!

It's not too late to slow climate change, but humans do need to change their behavior to accommodate so many extra people. We need to change the power sources we use, including using more solar and wind power and burning less fossil fuels. We also need to change how much energy we use at home, how we get around, and how we eat. Everyone working together will reduce the impact climate change has on our planet and on the millions of species, including humans, who share it.

WHAT CAN YOU DO?

Transportation

Reduce your greenhouse gases by changing the way you get around and flying less.

Walk or ride a bike—it's good for the planet, and it's healthy for you, too!

When walking or riding is not an option, try carpooling with friends or taking public transportation.

Not only do these reduce your greenhouse gas emissions, they can be fun!

Living

Changes in your home can make a big difference. Turn off the lights whenever you leave a room. Take shorter showers. Turn down the heat a couple of degrees. Seal the gaps around windows and doors. Use low-energy light bulbs such as LEDs.

In warmer months, close the window blinds and curtains to keep out the heat. Dry your clothes on a clothesline or rack instead of in the dryer.

Eating

Eating less meat (especially beef) and dairy foods will help reduce greenhouse gas emissions.

Try eating delicious and healthy vegetarian and vegan options each week.

Growing and transporting food to the store creates greenhouse gas emissions. Buying locally grown foods and wasting less food help.

Wasted food also produces methane, another greenhouse gas, when it rots.

Sharing

Talk with others about climate change and why it matters to everyone's future.

If enough of us talk to local, state, and federal leaders, we will make a really big impact. Call or write letters to your government leaders. Use social media, too (when you're old enough).

Get creative! Do a project or create art, a story, poem, song, dance, or play about climate change.

GLOSSARY

alpine – high in the mountains where it gets cold and snow can fall

breeding – mating to produce offspring (children)

carbon dioxide – gas made of one part carbon and two parts oxygen

climate change – a significant and long-term change in a place's usual weather, including temperature, precipitation, wind, humidity, and other factors

drought – period without rainfall or snowfall

elevation – height above sea level

forage – search for food

fossil fuel – fuel like oil, gas, or coal that comes from the long-ago remains of living things

greenhouse gas – gas such as carbon dioxide or methane that traps heat in the atmosphere

habitat – the usual environment in which a certain plant or animal lives

haypile – stash of plants a pika collects and stores under the rocks for winter food

hibernate – spend the winter in a resting state with a reduced heart rate and reduced body temperature

insulate – protect from heat or cold

methane – gas made of one part carbon and four parts hydrogen

migrate – move from one place to another, for example, leave a place that gets cold in winter to go to a warmer place

pollinator – animal such as a bee that brings pollen to a flower's egg cells so they can grow into seeds

precipitation – rain, sleet, hail, or snow

predator – animal that eats other animals

prey – animal that a predator eats

resource – something a living thing needs to survive, such as water or food

species – group of living things that are similar to each other and can breed with each other to produce offspring

To Dan Hartman, who inspired this book. —D.H.P.

To Sue and Ned for your unceasing support and belief in me. —M.G.

To the pikas, may they continue to survive. —D.H.

Special thanks to our teacher readers Karin Morris, Cindy Pfost, and
Luz Salazar and to scientists Shawn Morrison, Ph.D., and Clark Richards, Ph.D.,
for their invaluable expertise.

Text © 2020 by Dorothy Hinshaw Patent and Marlo Garnsworthy.
Photographs © 2020 by Daniel Hartman.
Graphics © 2020 by Marlo Garnsworthy.
Edited by Krista Faries.

Book design by Philip Krayna, Conifer Creative • www.conifercreative.com

For information, write to:
Web of Life Children's Books
P.O. Box 2726, Berkeley, California 94702

Published in the United States in 2020 by Web of Life Children's Books.

Library of Congress Control Number: 2019955522
ISBN 978-1-970039-02-3

Printed in China by Everbest Printing
Production Date: January 2020
Batch 86071

For more information about our books and the authors and artists who created them,
visit our website: www.weboflifebooks.com

Distributed by Publishers Group West/An Ingram Brand
(800)788-3123
www.pgw.com

FSC
www.fsc.org
MIX
Paper from
responsible sources
FSC® C124385

SPIDERS
NEAR AND FAR

JENNIFER OWINGS DEWEY

DUTTON CHILDREN'S BOOKS
NEW YORK

This book is dedicated to three new friends: Elise Noelle Alde, Molly Thorpe Talbert, and Dory Elizabeth Trimble—a new generation of spider lovers. And to my grandson, Kyle Loren Monroe Shaddeau.

Authorship is never a solitary endeavor. I owe special thanks to Dr. Donald Charles Lowrie, an adjunct curator of zoology at the New Mexico Museum of Natural History in Albuquerque, for his patience in going over this manuscript with me more than once. Dr. Lowrie, the author of numerous papers on spiders, and the discoverer of a few, is writing a book called *Spiders of New Mexico*. The book will be published by the museum.

Copyright © 1993 by Jennifer Owings Dewey

Library of Congress Cataloging-in-Publication Data

Dewey, Jennifer.
Spiders near and far/by Jennifer Owings Dewey.—1st ed.
p. cm.
Summary: Identifies the two major types of spiders and describes their body parts, behavior, and habitats.
ISBN 0-525-44979-5
1. Spiders—Juvenile literature. [1. Spiders.] I. Title.
QL458.4.D48 1993
595.4'4—dc20
92-6430 CIP AC

Published in the United States 1993 by
Dutton Children's Books,
a division of Penguin Books USA Inc.
375 Hudson Street, New York, New York 10014

Designed by Joseph Rutt

Printed in Hong Kong   First edition
10 9 8 7 6 5 4 3 2 1

A spider's scientific name consists of two words, usually Latin or latinized. The first word is the spider's genus, its main name. It is always capitalized. The second word names the spider's species, referring to its closest, most alike family relatives. That word is usually not capitalized.

Spider sizes given in this book represent an approximate measurement from foot tip to foot tip.

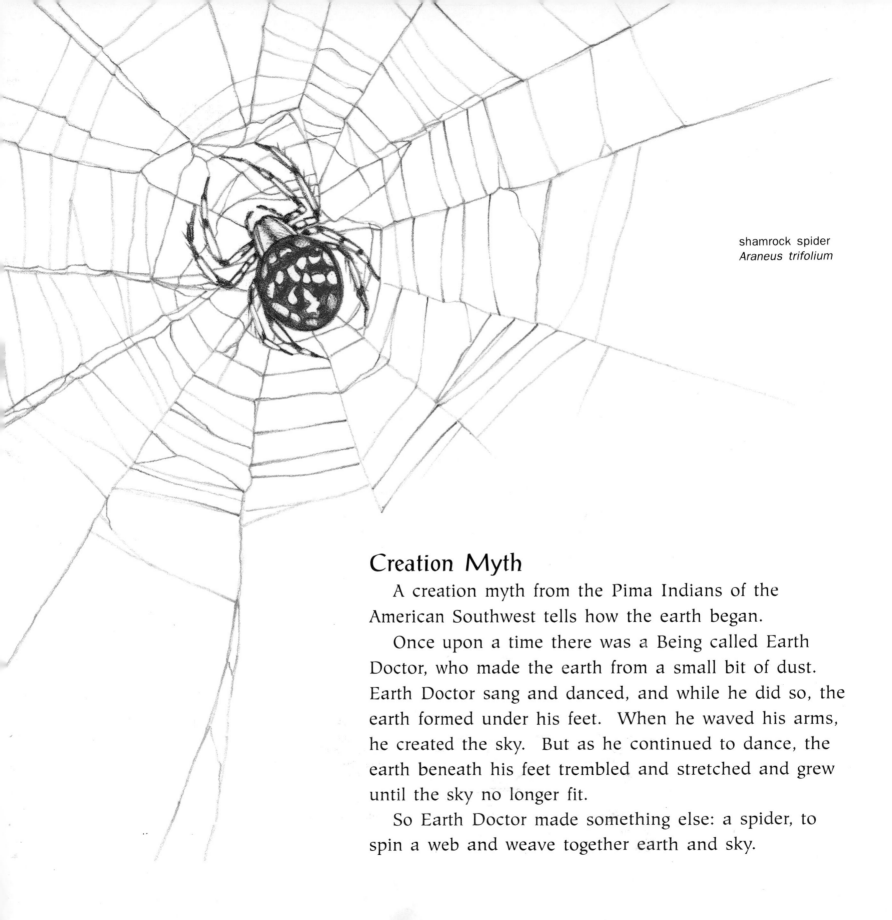

shamrock spider
Araneus trifolium

Creation Myth

A creation myth from the Pima Indians of the American Southwest tells how the earth began.

Once upon a time there was a Being called Earth Doctor, who made the earth from a small bit of dust. Earth Doctor sang and danced, and while he did so, the earth formed under his feet. When he waved his arms, he created the sky. But as he continued to dance, the earth beneath his feet trembled and stretched and grew until the sky no longer fit.

So Earth Doctor made something else: a spider, to spin a web and weave together earth and sky.

black-and-yellow argiope
Argiope aurantia

What Is a Spider?

Spiders live almost everywhere on earth, from seashores, swamps, and jungles to subways, basements, and shopping centers. Spiders live as near to you as the corner of your clothes closet or the drain in your bathtub. They also live as far from you as the Arctic tundra or the slopes of Mount Everest. Young spiders have even been discovered floating on air currents sixteen thousand feet above the earth.

Those who study spiders are careful as to what general statements they make about them. This is because spider behavior can vary from one part of the world to another. Two spiders of exactly the same kind may behave differently if one lives in Montana and the other lives in Moscow. Close observation of spiders in their natural environments is the best way to come to know them.

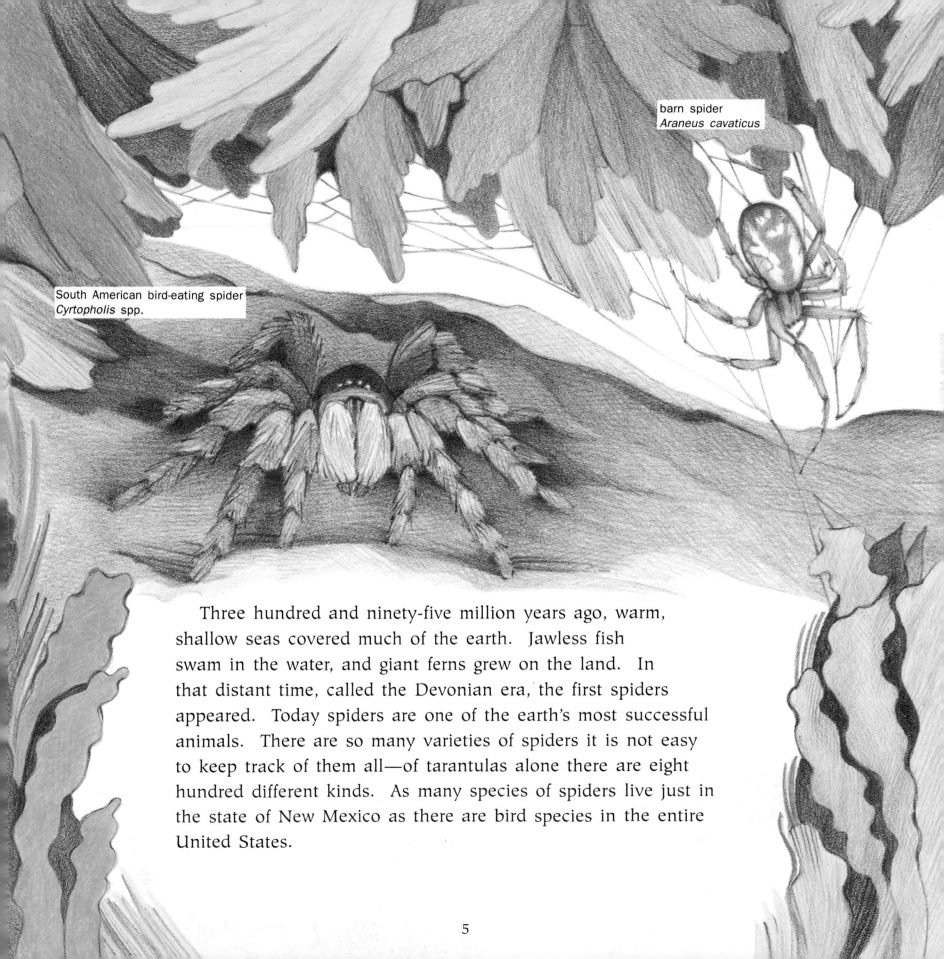

barn spider
Araneus cavaticus

South American bird-eating spider
Cyrtopholis spp.

Three hundred and ninety-five million years ago, warm, shallow seas covered much of the earth. Jawless fish swam in the water, and giant ferns grew on the land. In that distant time, called the Devonian era, the first spiders appeared. Today spiders are one of the earth's most successful animals. There are so many varieties of spiders it is not easy to keep track of them all—of tarantulas alone there are eight hundred different kinds. As many species of spiders live just in the state of New Mexico as there are bird species in the entire United States.

Spiders are not insects, though their jointed legs make them look as though they were. Spider bodies and insect bodies are different in important ways. Spiders have eight legs, while insects have six. Spiders have only two distinct body parts; insects have three. All insects have antennae and most have at least one pair of wings, but spiders have no wings and no antennae. Only spiders have silk glands and spinnerets at the rear of their abdomens.

Spiders belong to a group called Arachnida, animals with four pairs of legs, no antennae or wings, and only two body parts. Scorpions, mites, and daddy longlegs are other arachnids. They are cousins of spiders, but they are not spiders.

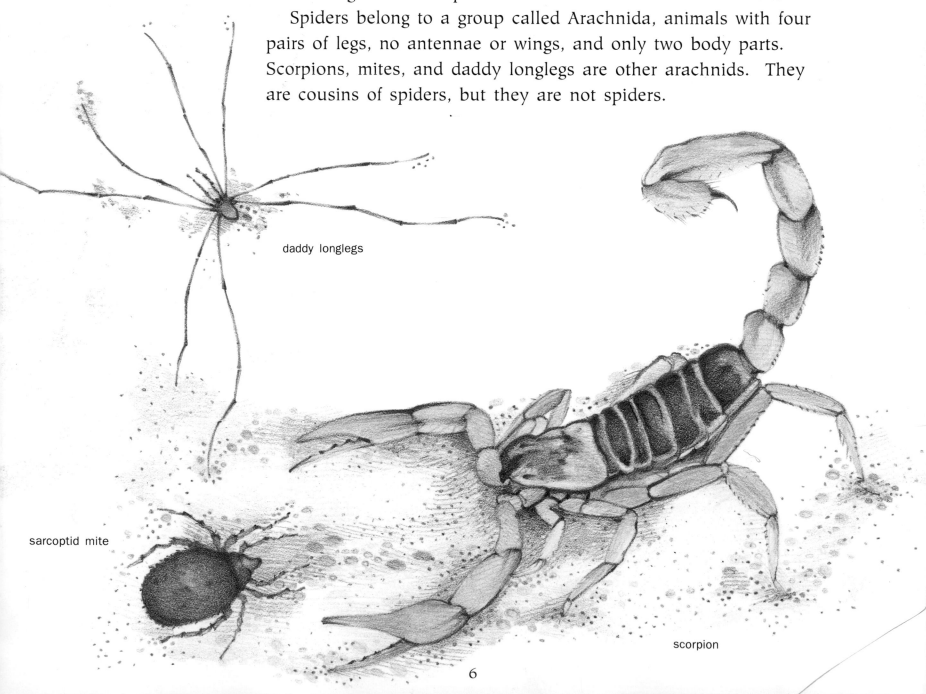

daddy longlegs

sarcoptid mite

scorpion

6

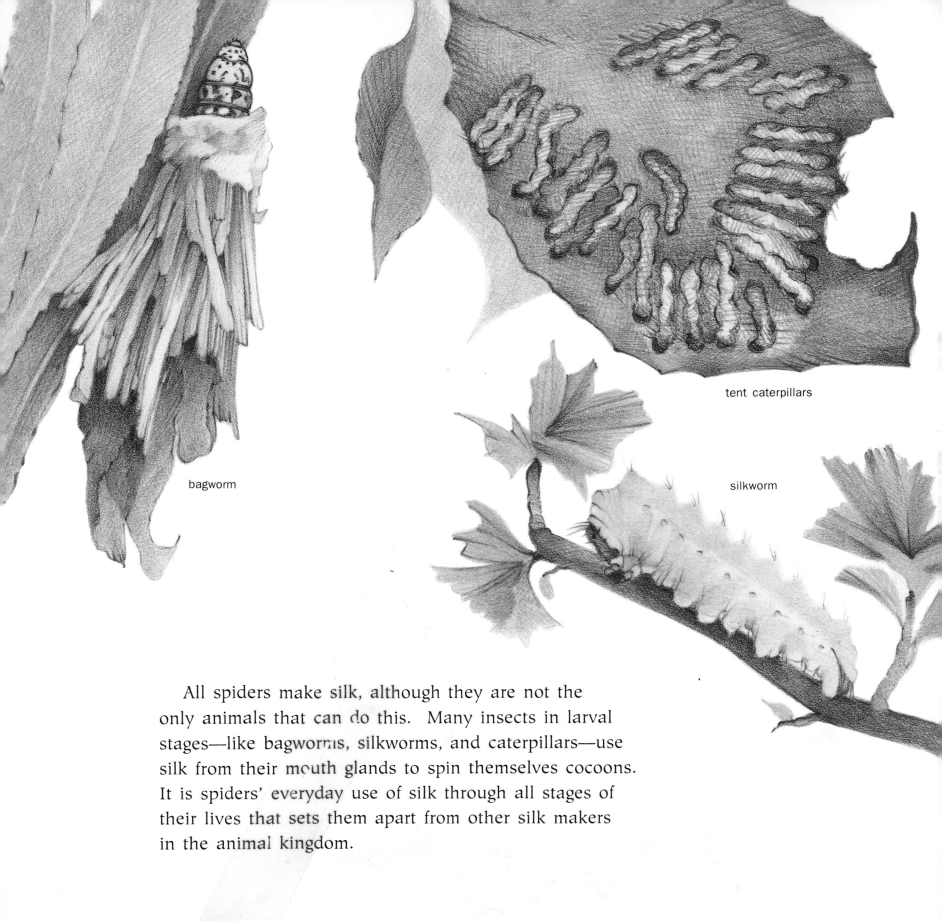

bagworm

tent caterpillars

silkworm

   All spiders make silk, although they are not the
only animals that can do this. Many insects in larval
stages—like bagworms, silkworms, and caterpillars—use
silk from their mouth glands to spin themselves cocoons.
It is spiders' everyday use of silk through all stages of
their lives that sets them apart from other silk makers
in the animal kingdom.

There are two basic kinds of spiders:
web builders and wanderers. Web builders
spin webs and silken traps to catch their prey.
They spend most of their lives in one place,
never traveling far.

banded argiope
Argiope trifasciata

desert tarantula
Aphonopelma chalcodes

Wandering spiders are nomads, moving from place to
place, searching for insects to eat. Some sit and wait,
but most wanderers are free-roving hunters, chasing
down prey and pouncing to make a kill.

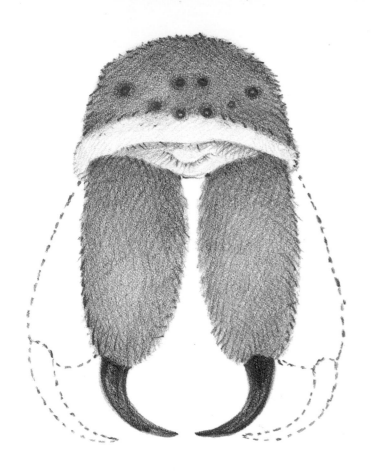

spider jaw parts swing from side to side

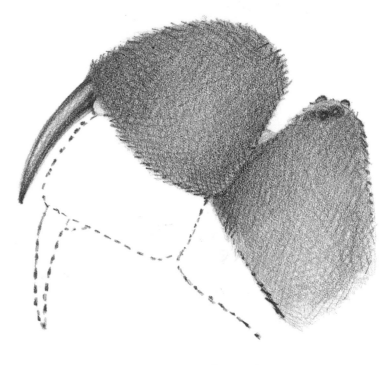

extended fang, raised to stab prey

To subdue and kill its prey, a spider bites with its strong jaws. The jaws are equipped with sharp fangs that can pierce an insect's hard outer covering. When the spider's paralyzing venom, or poison, flows through its fangs, the struggling insect, often much bigger than the attacking spider, is quickly stilled. Not all spiders have poison glands, though most do. The potency of the venom varies from spider to spider.

All spiders are carnivores—animals that eat other animals. But most spiders do not chew, so they live on liquid diets. Digestive juices in a spider's venom liquefy an insect's insides, and the spider sucks the fluid out.

banded argiope
Argiope trifasciata

Silk

Spiders depend on their silk much the way we humans depend on our arms, legs, and hands. Silk is the material spiders use to spin webs, traps, anchor lines, egg sacs, burrow linings, and tents. Whether a spider lives in a remote tropical jungle or under a park bench in Chicago, silk is essential to its survival.

Like human hair, silk is a protein. It comes from glands inside a spider's body. Some spiders have two silk glands, while others have five or even seven. The glands are connected to a number of small raised openings, the spinnerets, at the tip of a spider's abdomen.

Each silk gland makes a different kind of silk: fuzzy or smooth, thick or thin, dry or sticky. A spider spins whatever type of silk is best for the task at hand. Web builders, for instance, spin extrastrong silk as foundation lines for their webs; they spin sticky silk for the centers of their webs.

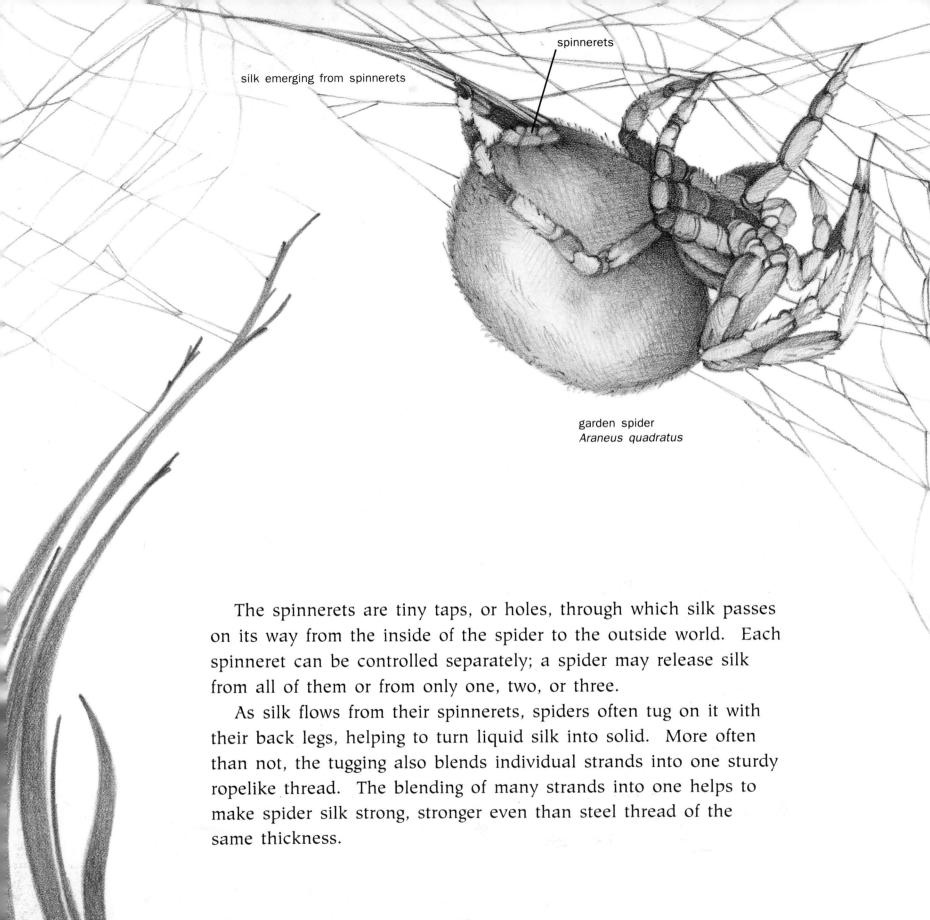

spinnerets

silk emerging from spinnerets

garden spider
Araneus quadratus

The spinnerets are tiny taps, or holes, through which silk passes on its way from the inside of the spider to the outside world. Each spinneret can be controlled separately; a spider may release silk from all of them or from only one, two, or three.

As silk flows from their spinnerets, spiders often tug on it with their back legs, helping to turn liquid silk into solid. More often than not, the tugging also blends individual strands into one sturdy ropelike thread. The blending of many strands into one helps to make spider silk strong, stronger even than steel thread of the same thickness.

A Spider's Body

A spider's eyes, mouth, brains, stomach, and poison glands are all in the smaller of its two body parts. This part is called the cephalothorax. It can be thought of as the spider's chest and head.

Most spiders have eight eyes, but some have two and others four or six. Regardless of how many, spiders tend not to see very well. Wandering spiders, who use their eyes for hunting, see a little better than web builders. Stay-at-home web builders, who wait for prey to get stuck in their webs, see poorly or not at all.

The larger part of a spider's body contains its reproductive organs, digestive tract, heart, lungs, and silk glands. This part is called the abdomen. In some spiders the abdomen becomes very large as the spider ages. A thin stalk contains muscles, nerves, and the intestine. Called the pedicel, it is a connecting channel between the abdomen and the cephalothorax.

As spiders grow, they molt, or shed their outer skin. When a skin is too small, it splits, and the spider crawls out of it. Within hours, a new, properly fitting skin hardens in place of the old.

top view

eyes

abdomen

cephalothorax

garden spider
Araneus quadratus

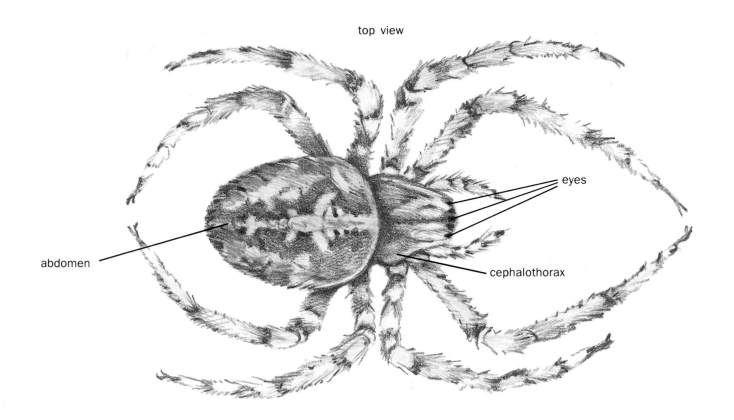

bottom view

pedicel

fangs

spinnerets

jaws

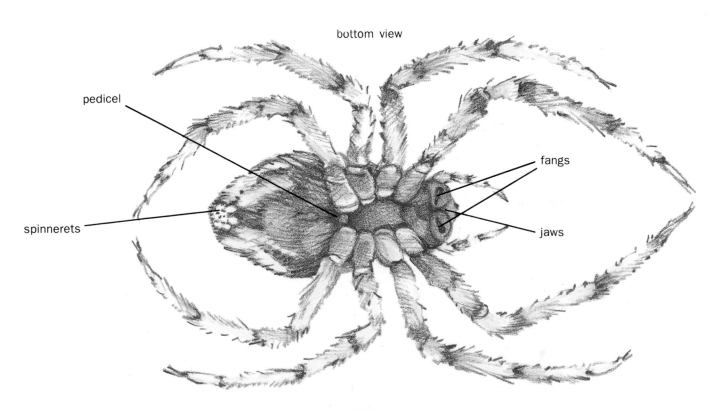

black-and-yellow argiope
Argiope aurantia

black widow
Latrodectus mactans

Web Builders—Orb Weavers

A spider spins a web to catch food, much the way people fishing use a net to catch fish. The shape of a web and where it is spun are clues to what sort of web builder made it.

If you took the time to search one acre of meadow, you might find as many as two million wheel-shaped webs strung in the grass. These are the webs of orb weavers. Orb weavers live everywhere except Antarctica, spinning their silk into lacy, circular constructions.

golden silk spider
Nephila clavipes

Female orb weavers are the web builders; if you see an orb weaver spinning a web, it is the female you are watching. Their webs can be wide enough to straddle a small stream or as small as the center of a daisy.

A kind of orb weaver called *Nephila* lives in warm countries all over the world. In the South Sea Islands, high in leafy branches, *Nephila* spins a web eight to ten feet across. She is called the golden silk spider because her web of golden silk matches the gold patches on her back. The silk webbing is so sturdy that South Sea Islanders collect it to weave into bags, floor mats, and fishing nets.

15

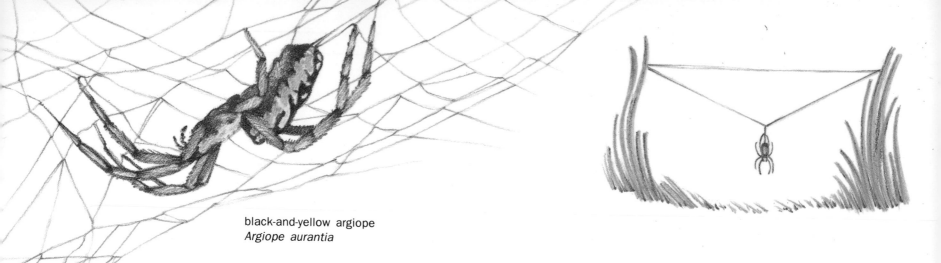

black-and-yellow argiope
Argiope aurantia

An American garden spider, the inch-long orb weaver called *Argiope aurantia,* spins her webs in fields, especially along the edges of ditches and ponds, where flying insects gather. She also chooses shadowy corners under porches or deep recesses of window frames for her weavings.

Argiope aurantia's body is shiny black with orange or yellow blotches. The web she builds is tough and elastic, strong enough to capture a bee. If bad weather or the struggles of an insect damage the web beyond repair, she simply spins a new web in the same spot as the old. Many orb weavers eat their old webs, thus recycling the protein. Some just make repairs.

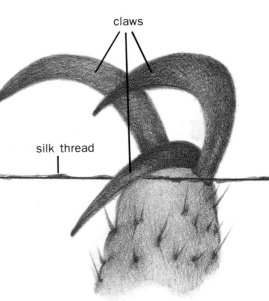

claws

silk thread

orb-weaver foot

Argiope begins a web by grasping a twig or a blade of grass and raising her abdomen in the air. Through her spinnerets she emits strands of silk that merge and become a single thread. Holding the thread close to her body with her back legs, she allows the free end to drift away. She releases more silk as needed, and finally the free end touches something, a stem or flower stalk. It is a contact point.

Spinning more silk, the spider sets to work on the circular shape that will become her web. She starts with triangles of lines, called bridge lines, on which she will walk from one section of the web to another. Orb weavers have three claws on each foot, unlike most spiders, which have only two. The extra claw helps the spider manipulate her web threads.

When the bridge lines are in place, she spins sticky silk to form the spiral center of the web. Spider experts disagree on how the spider avoids getting stuck in her own sticky silk. Some believe a substance on her body keeps the spider free. Others suggest the spider wets her feet with a solution produced in her mouth, an "oil" that resists stickiness.

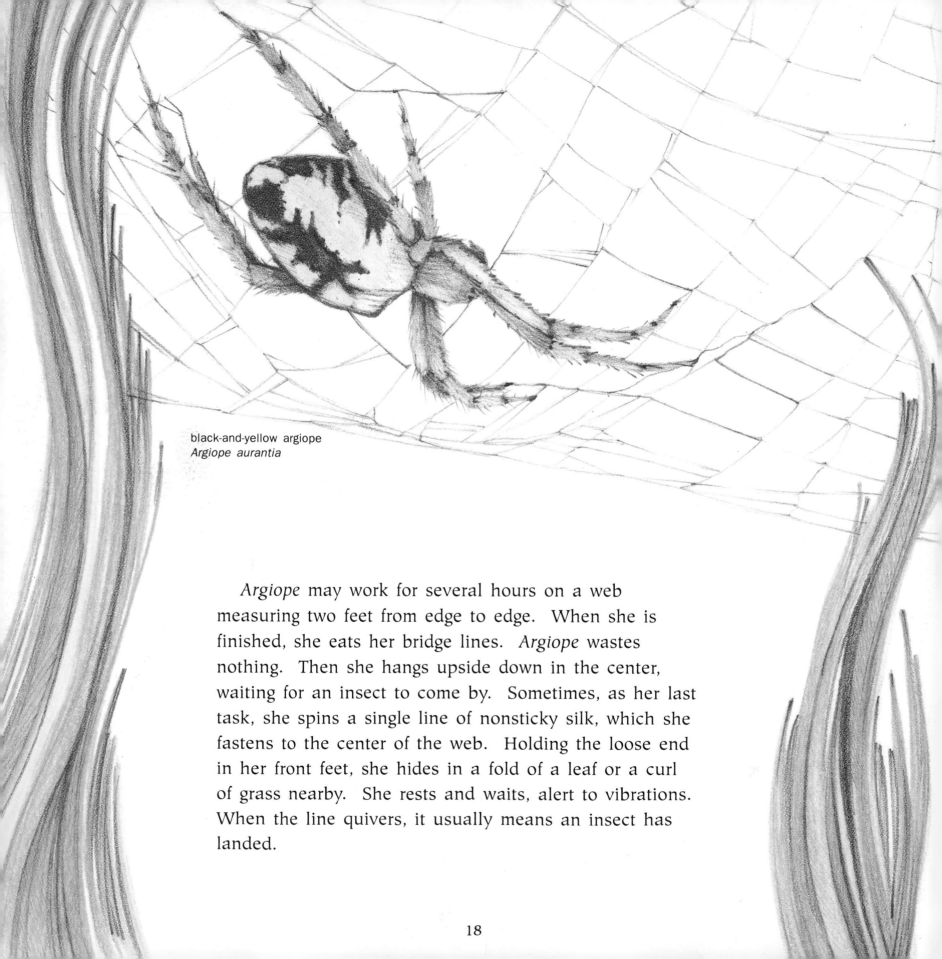

black-and-yellow argiope
Argiope aurantia

Argiope may work for several hours on a web measuring two feet from edge to edge. When she is finished, she eats her bridge lines. *Argiope* wastes nothing. Then she hangs upside down in the center, waiting for an insect to come by. Sometimes, as her last task, she spins a single line of nonsticky silk, which she fastens to the center of the web. Holding the loose end in her front feet, she hides in a fold of a leaf or a curl of grass nearby. She rests and waits, alert to vibrations. When the line quivers, it usually means an insect has landed.

When you next see an orb weaver's web, gently pluck a web strand or two with a twig. The spider may scamper out on her web, as she would do if you were an insect landing. Orb weavers rely on a keen sense of touch to know what goes on around them. Movement on their lines, not what they see, brings them out from hiding.

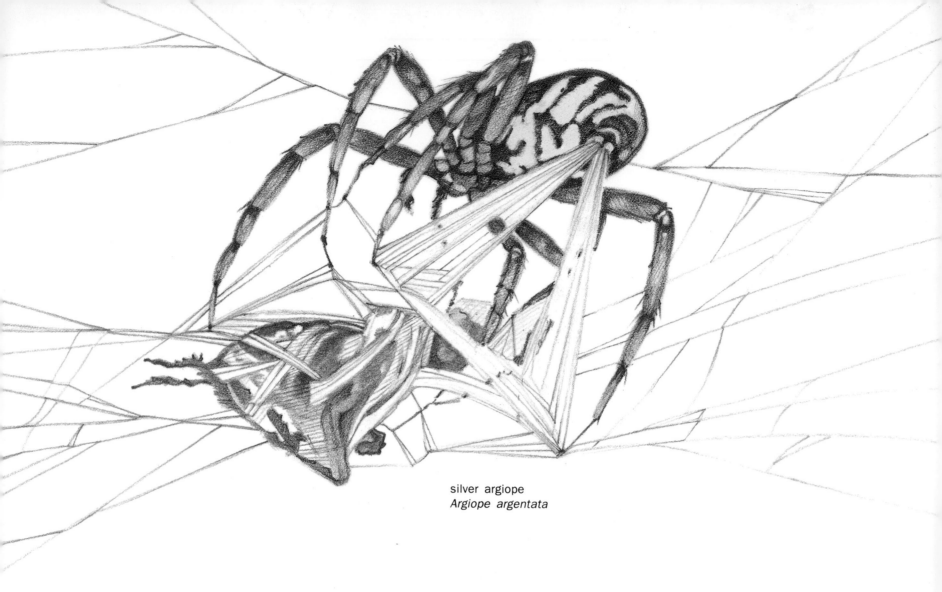

silver argiope
Argiope argentata

When an insect, such as a grasshopper, runs into an orb weaver's web, its violent thrashing jerks the line. In a split second the spider is out and has paralyzed her victim with her bite.

Turning her belly to the grasshopper, she releases a stream of sticky threads through her spinnerets. She may use all of them at once to produce a lot of silk. With her back legs, she gathers up the flow and flings it over her prey, trapping it in a gluey bandage.

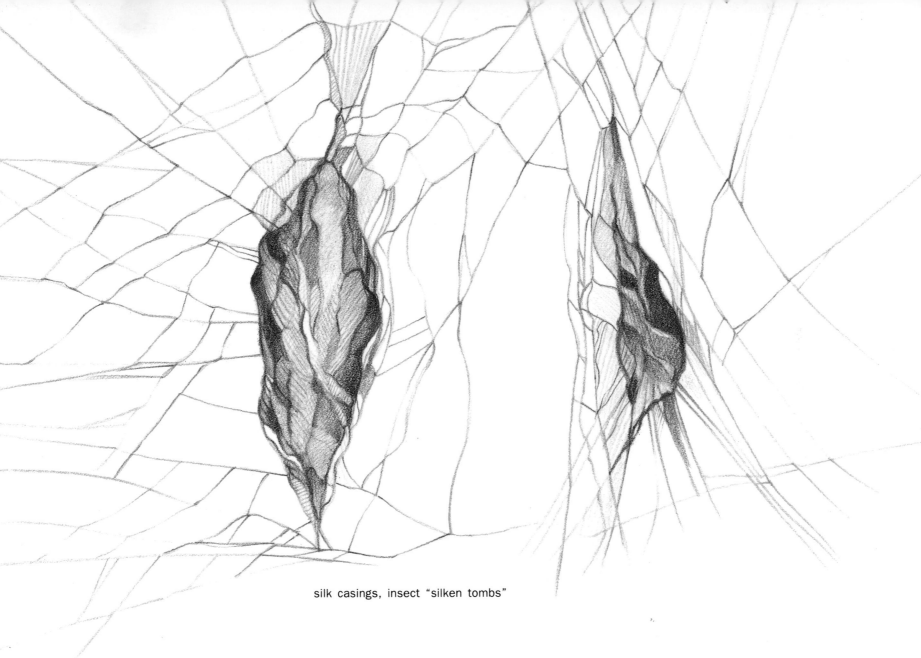

silk casings, insect "silken tombs"

A quick stab or stabs with needle-sharp fangs, a spurt of venom into the grasshopper's nerves and muscles, and the insect is unconscious. The spider sucks out the contents of the grasshopper's body, leaving only its hard exoskeleton enclosed in a silken tomb. Sometimes you can see these leftovers, known as silk casings, hanging on the webs of orb weavers. The cases are different sizes, depending on what insect was wrapped inside.

21

carrion beetle

funnel web of
Agelena naevia

Other Web Builders—
Curious Snares, Unusual Traps

A carrion beetle walking in a field of oats tumbles into the sticky meshlike webbing of a funnel weaver. A red-and-black harlequin beetle, creeping over rough lava rock, meets a similar fate when it steps into the gluey layered web of a desert-dwelling funnel weaver.

Male and female funnel weavers build funnel-shaped webs, spinning their webs on the ground, often around the bases of trees or rocks or in grassy fields. These spiders are quick moving and small, usually less than one inch across. They live all over the world, in orchards, vacant lots, deserts, and forests, on mountainsides and beaches.

Australian funnel web spider
Atrax robustus

One of the world's biggest spiders, *Atrax robustus,* is four inches wide and lives in Australia. It builds a funnel web, although it is considered a tarantula relative, not a relative of other funnel-web builders. Its huge fangs can pierce a human finger. A victim suffers violent twitching and heavy sweating and may even die.

funnel web spider
Agelena naevia

A smaller funnel weaver called *Agelena naevia* spins a web that looks like a lace napkin. Its fine layers of silk can form a sheet on grass, stones, or bark, or across cracks in rocks.

Somewhere on *Agelena*'s sheetlike web is a small but deep funnel shape. The spider hides in this little cave, waiting for an insect to pass by and trip on the sticky threads. A locust stumbling into *Agelena*'s web quickly finds itself entangled. It cannot jump free. *Agelena* attacks by springing from her hole and stabbing her fangs into the victim. She drags the paralyzed insect back to her funnel and drains it dry, later tossing the insect's remains beyond the edges of the web.

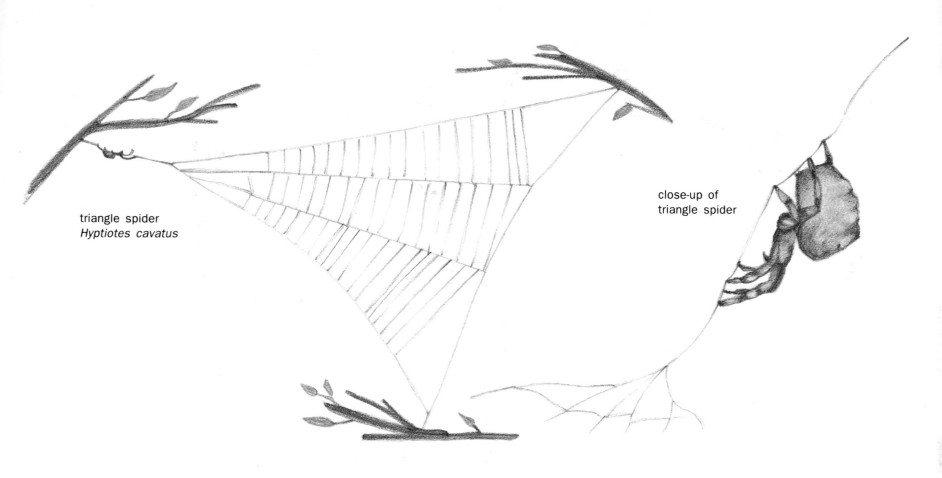

triangle spider
Hyptiotes cavatus

close-up of
triangle spider

    Hyptiotes, the triangle spider, has a slender brown body about one inch long. It is a hard spider to find because it stays hidden under piles of leaves or in grassy, mossy patches on the ground. It spins a triangular web, attaching a long thread to one point of the triangle. With its four front legs, it pulls the thread tight.

    The moment an insect lands on the web, the spider lunges forward in the direction of its catch. The web's tension is released, and the insect's legs become tangled in a mass of sticky threads. Then the spider attacks, sinking sharp fangs into its prey.

    The triangle spider sucks its prey dry, then eats the old web. It will spin a new web when it is ready to capture another insect.

Comb-footed spiders, or cobweb weavers, are common all over the world. These spiders spin webs indoors or outdoors, in attics or cellars, in shoe boxes or under fallen logs. Cobweb weavers choose dark, secluded places for their webs, like woodpiles or the spaces between loose bricks. They hang upside down in the center of their webs, waiting for insects to happen along.

Comb-footed spiders have eight or ten bristles, lined up like a comb, on each of their four back legs. They use the bristles to comb and stroke their silk as it flows from their spinnerets. Combed silk turns back on itself and looks stringy. Cobwebs appear messy and fragile, but they are efficient traps for insects. The tangle of threads makes escape difficult once an insect blunders in.

close-up of black widow's comb foot

black-widow web

black widow
Latrodectus mactans

The best-known cobweb weavers, and the biggest,
are the widows, named for their tendency to "widow"
themselves by eating their mates. (The males are small
and do not construct cobwebs.) The black widow,
Latrodectus mactans, lives in North and South America.
On the spider's underside, a brilliant hourglass pattern of
red or orange makes her easy to identify. The black of a
black widow often shines in the sun like polished leather.

Although many spider bites reported in North America
are widow bites, these spiders are not aggressive and
would sooner hide from people than bite them. The bite
causes the tissues around the wound to die, and it takes
a long time to heal. The potency of black-widow venom
can cause death in babies, small children, or sickly
adults. Bites must be taken seriously and treated by
a doctor.

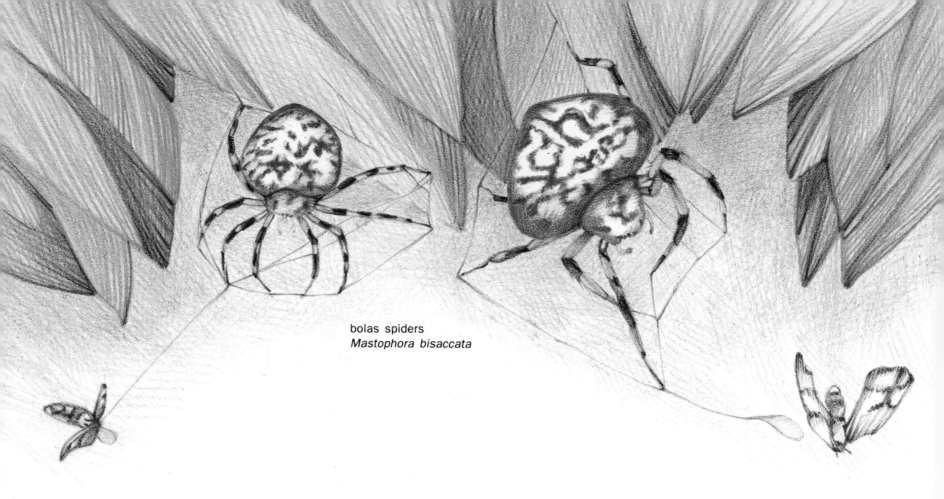

bolas spiders
Mastophora bisaccata

The bolas spider, *Mastophora bisaccata*, lives in lush flower gardens in Asia, Europe, and the southeastern United States. Red, orange, and black, half an inch long, it hangs from a twig or a stem and spins a sticky line of silk. To the end of the line it attaches a silky wad saturated with a pheromone, a chemical that attracts moths, made in a gland in the spider's body.

Bolas is a Spanish word for "ball," which well describes the spider's gummy wad. Hunting at twilight, when night-flying moths are out and about, the spider swings its line, much the way a cowboy swings a lasso. Moths are drawn to the odor of the ball, and there they become stuck, unable to fly free. The spider hauls in the line and eats.

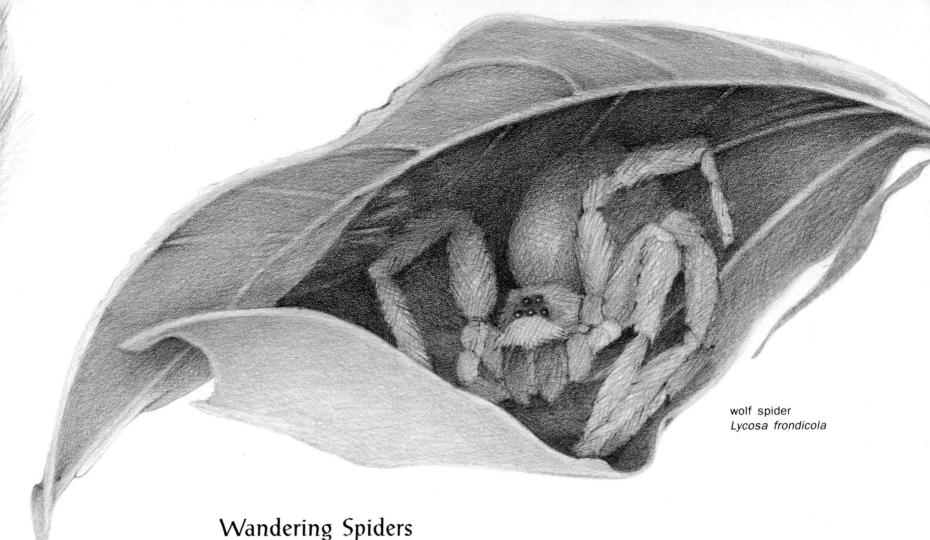

wolf spider
Lycosa frondicola

Wandering Spiders

Wandering spiders live nomadic lives, hunting, stalking, lunging at insect prey. Males and females spin silk, but not for webs that snare and trap. They use their silk for burrow linings, anchor lines, or egg sacs. Though a wandering spider uses less silk than a web builder, silk is still crucial to its survival.

Wolf spiders are wandering spiders named for their hairy bodies and their habit of running swiftly over the ground. Despite the name, wolf spiders are solitary and hunt alone, not in packs like true wolves. They can be quite large or very small, and sometimes their hairs are hard to see.

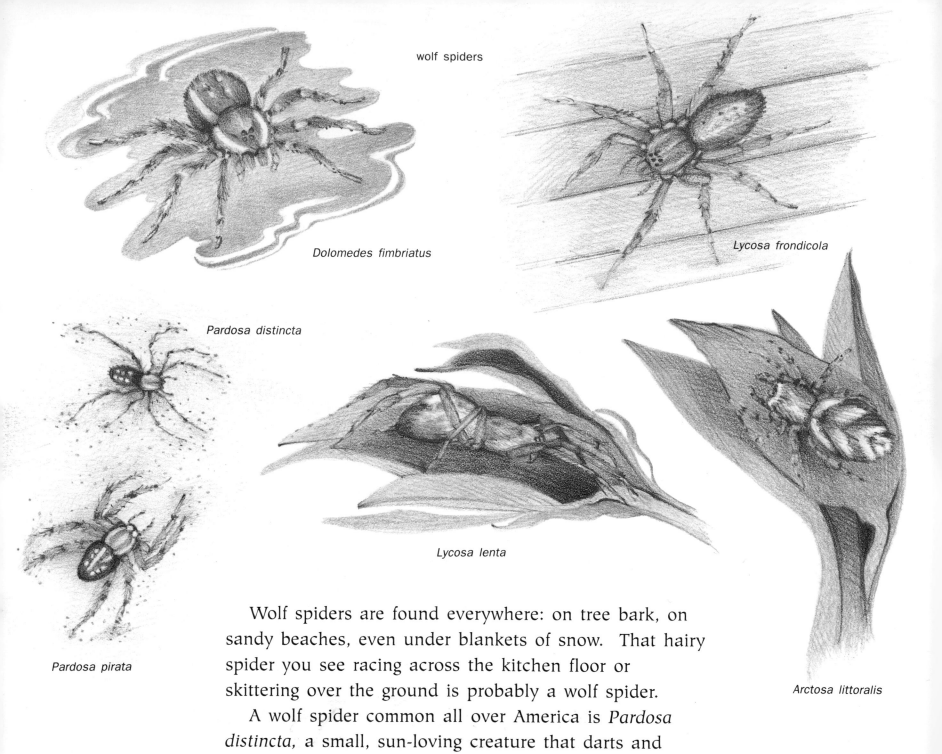

wolf spiders

Dolomedes fimbriatus

Lycosa frondicola

Pardosa distincta

Pardosa pirata

Lycosa lenta

Arctosa littoralis

Wolf spiders are found everywhere: on tree bark, on sandy beaches, even under blankets of snow. That hairy spider you see racing across the kitchen floor or skittering over the ground is probably a wolf spider.

A wolf spider common all over America is *Pardosa distincta,* a small, sun-loving creature that darts and dashes wherever it goes. The pirate wolf spider, *Pardosa pirata,* can be found near ponds and streams. It is able to run across water without falling in, because of water-repellent hairs on its feet.

tree frog

South American bird-eating spider
Cyrtopholis spp.

Another hairy wandering spider, the tarantula, was once thought to be a wolf spider. However, people who study spiders now agree that tarantulas belong to a distinct family of spiders unrelated to wolf spiders. Tarantulas are usually large, with leg spans of five or six inches. *Cyrtopholis,* a tarantula that lives in South American rain forests, climbs trees and captures tree frogs. The pads of hair on its feet make it a good climber.

Most American tarantulas are smaller than their South American cousins, with leg spans of two to four inches, although some southwestern desert tarantulas reach six inches in width. American tarantulas live in hot, dry places and dig burrows that they line with silk. Their bite is no worse for a person than a wasp or bee sting. Female tarantulas tend to live long lives, some as long as twenty years.

An American desert tarantula, *Aphonopelma chalcodes*, makes a silk-lined burrow in sandy soil. It sleeps all day and crawls out at night to hunt. Peering into the darkness with eight greenish eyes, it searches for lizards, insects, and small mammals. Sensitive hairs on the spider's legs detect vibrations from other moving creatures. Once it senses and sees a possible victim, the spider gives chase, jumping to make a kill.

In the American Southwest, groups of tarantulas crossing highways often alarm drivers. They may have emerged from their burrows in search of water, or they may be males in search of females. It is fascinating to watch these big hairy spiders marching over the ground, but it is best to leave them undisturbed. Tarantulas are essentially harmless to humans, and they eat many of the insects people consider pests.

desert tarantulas
Aphonopelma chalcodes

trap-door spider
Bothriocyrtum californicum

   With their thick legs and hairy bodies, trap-door spiders resemble tarantulas, but they are not tarantulas. Their bodies are longer and narrower. Their legs are often short and stumpy. They live in warm deserts and the tropics.

   An American trap-door spider, *Bothriocyrtum californicum*, lives in the deserts of southern California. It is a favorite of spider collectors because it is easy to find. Its dark burrow lid shows up plainly on the desert sand.

The California trap-door spider digs a tubelike burrow in sandy soil, sometimes as deep as twelve inches. To dig, it uses special rakes on its jaws. The spider seals its burrow with a hinged lid that it makes from soil, silk, and saliva. Then it sits in its burrow, holding the door shut with its fangs. When it senses the vibrations of approaching prey, the spider pops open the lid, bites its victim, and pulls it in to feed.

trap-door spider in burrow and capturing centipede

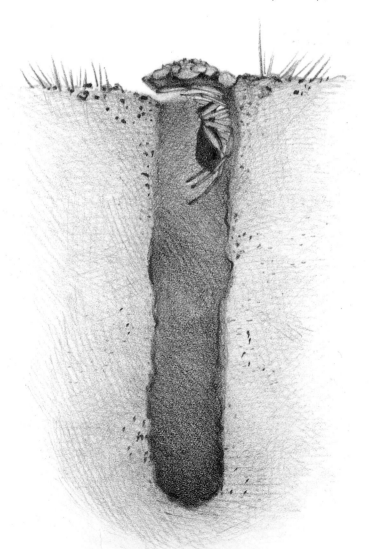
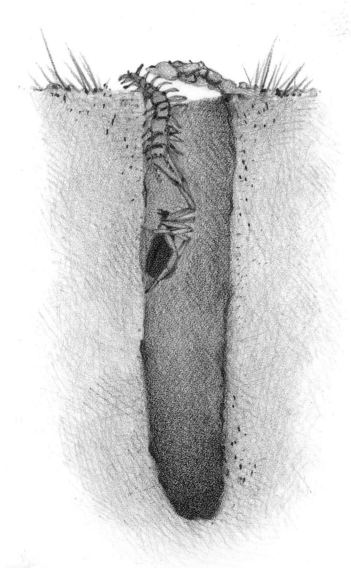

Another wandering spider, one that spits, lives throughout the world—in houses and apartments and also in grassy, weedy places like pastures and meadows. The brownish orange *Scytodes thoracica* has a unique way of snaring a victim.

Hiding under piles of leaves or dead grass, the spitting spider keeps perfectly still. When an insect passes nearby, the spider fires a sticky substance from its fangs over the victim's body. The material is wet with venom, so the insect is trapped under a gooey net. Then the spider rushes at the struggling insect and pierces it with sharp fangs.

spitting spider
Scytodes thoracica

Thomisidae, a family of wandering spiders, are known as crab spiders. A crab spider not only resembles the shape of a crab, it also crawls backward and sideways like a crab.

Crab spiders live all over the world, on plants, flowers, and tree bark. Some live on the ground, under leaves and twigs. When you walk in the woods, look closely at bushes and wildflowers. You may catch sight of these small crablike spiders staring back at you.

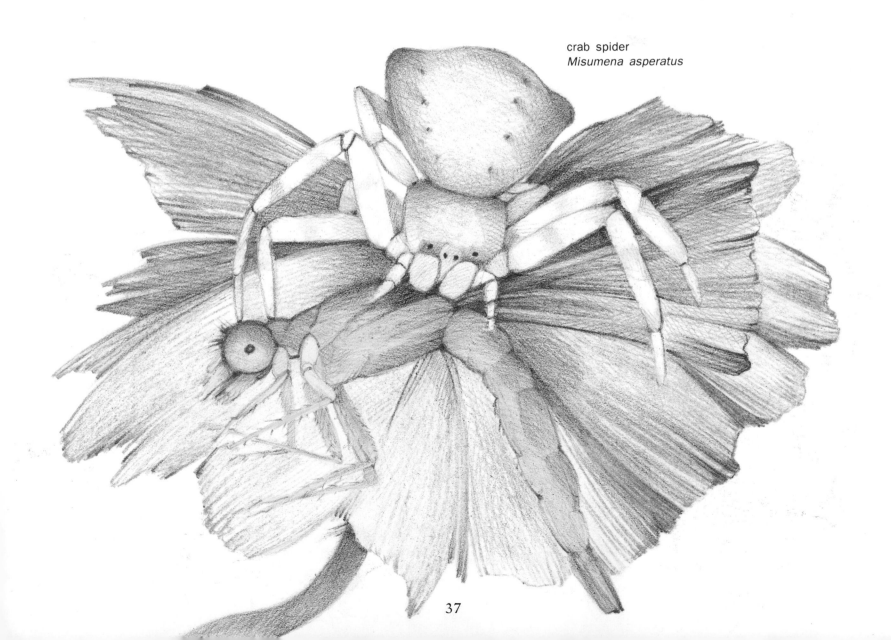

crab spider
Misumena asperatus

crab spiders
Misumena spp.

Sitting on a flower or a tree branch, a dime-sized crab spider waits in ambush. Quick to detect movement, the spider lunges when an insect comes close. It grabs the prey with its front legs and bites it. Crab-spider venom is especially potent, able to bring down a bee, butterfly, or beetle two or three times larger than the spider itself.

Some crab-spider colors blend perfectly with flower
colors and patterns. Among yellow flowers you will find
yellow crab spiders; on pink flowers, pink ones. When
a flower dies, the spider simply moves to another one.
Crab spiders on tree bark are bark colored, and those
on the ground are dull gray or brown.

Like crab spiders, jumping spiders, of the family Salticidae, are wanderers that move fast and have relatively superior vision. Most jumping spiders are less than half an inch long. All are brightly colored—orange, red, yellow, or silver—and all have the best vision in the spider world.

Jumpers stalk their prey, using their excellent eyesight, jumping for a capture at the last second. They are able to jump twenty times their own length.

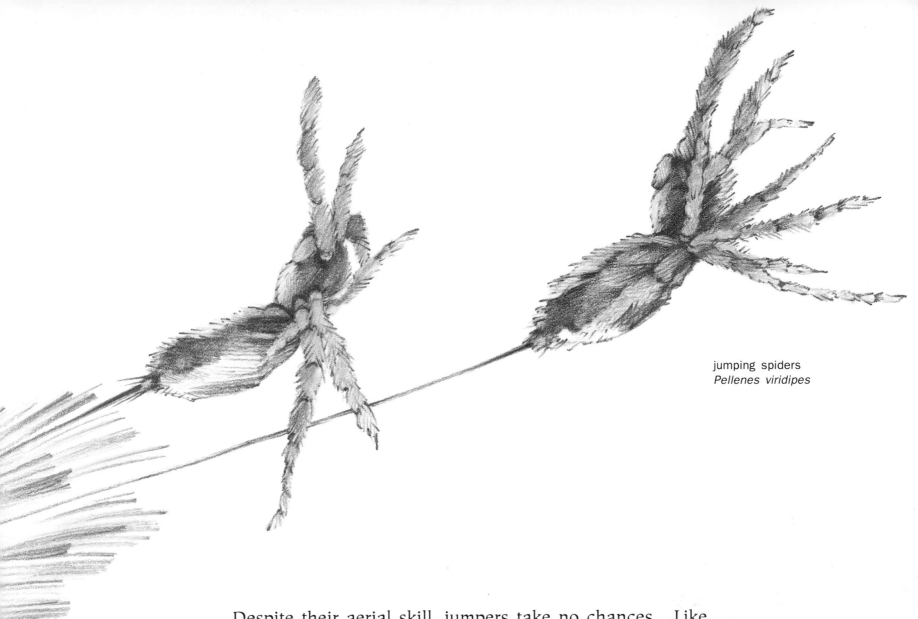

jumping spiders
Pellenes viridipes

Despite their aerial skill, jumpers take no chances. Like mountain climbers with ropes, they release safety lines of silk with every leap. The line helps control the spider's fall through space.

Jumpers live all over the world, in warm climates and in harsh ones, too. They have even been found on the slopes of mountains twenty thousand feet high, where the air is cold and thin. If you see a hairy little spider, brilliantly colored and with beady eyes, clinging to a screen door or drainpipe, it is most likely a jumping spider.

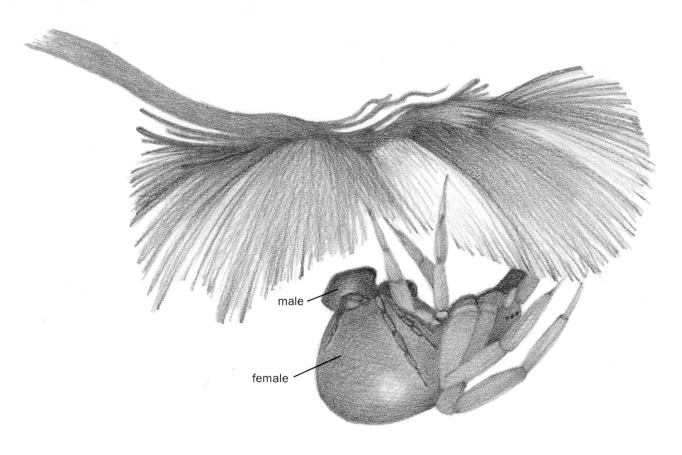

male

female

crab spiders *(Misumena vatia)* mating

Mating

Mating behavior among spiders is nearly as varied as spiders themselves. A common problem for a male spider ready to mate is the voracious appetite of the female. Any creature approaching a female spider, including a male of her own kind, is a potential meal. Whether web builder or wanderer, a hungry female is more likely to attack a male than welcome him.

If mating is successful, and the male escapes the lethal fangs of the female, he soon dies anyway, having fulfilled his role.

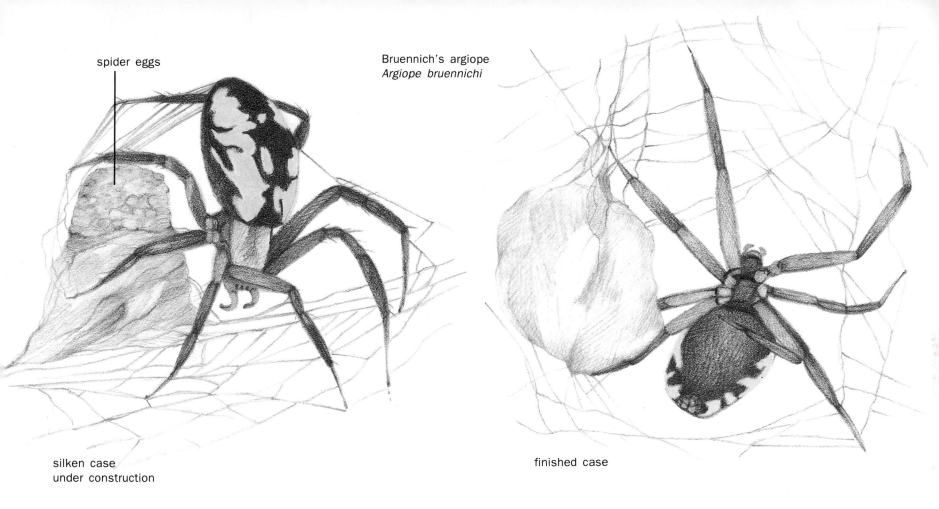

spider eggs

Bruennich's argiope
Argiope bruennichi

silken case
under construction

finished case

Eggs and Egg Sacs

Spider silk, so important to a spider's life, is crucial at egg-laying time, when the spider uses it to spin a container for her eggs. A female begins her egg sac by spinning a disk of silk. Then she lays her eggs. As the eggs emerge from her body, their "skin" hardens, helping to protect them. Still, the eggs are very delicate. When all the eggs are laid on the disk, the female spins enough silk to surround them, shaping a protective bundlelike sac. Silk used to cushion the eggs is the finest a spider spins.

The number of eggs a spider lays is related to her size. Large spiders tend to lay more eggs than small spiders. Black widows, relatively large spiders, lay up to a thousand eggs.

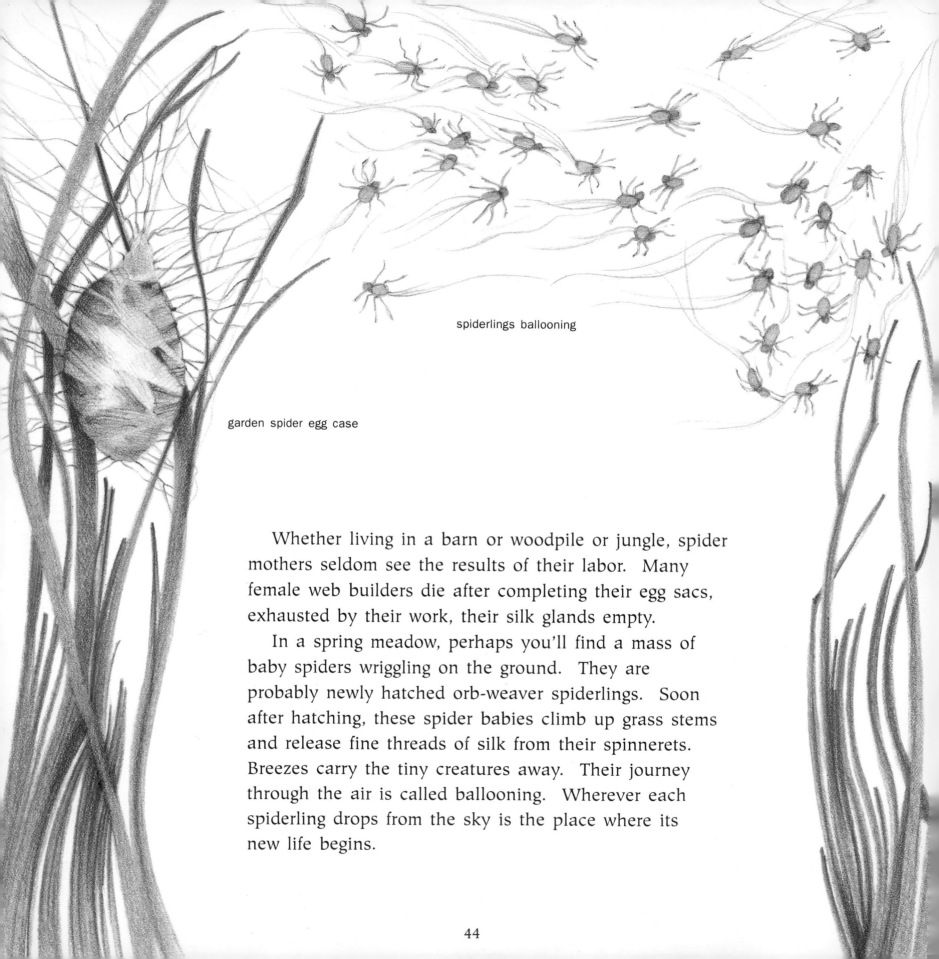

spiderlings ballooning

garden spider egg case

Whether living in a barn or woodpile or jungle, spider mothers seldom see the results of their labor. Many female web builders die after completing their egg sacs, exhausted by their work, their silk glands empty.

In a spring meadow, perhaps you'll find a mass of baby spiders wriggling on the ground. They are probably newly hatched orb-weaver spiderlings. Soon after hatching, these spider babies climb up grass stems and release fine threads of silk from their spinnerets. Breezes carry the tiny creatures away. Their journey through the air is called ballooning. Wherever each spiderling drops from the sky is the place where its new life begins.

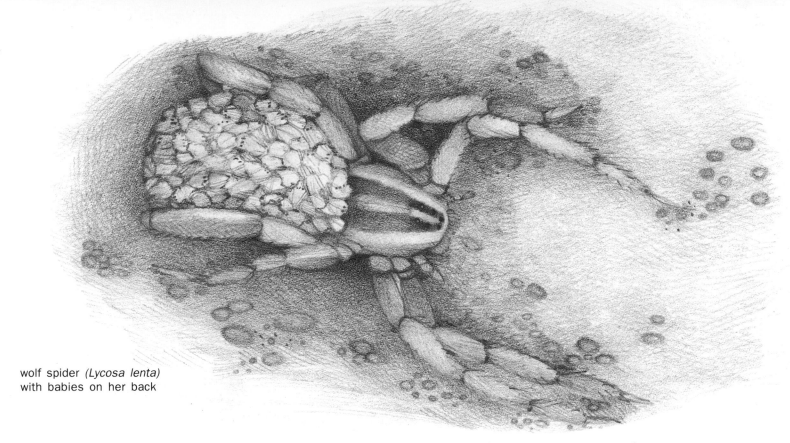

wolf spider *(Lycosa lenta)*
with babies on her back

Wolf spiders, on the other hand, tie their egg sacs to their bodies with silk lines. When the spiderlings are ready to hatch, the mother spider chews a hole in the sac, helping them emerge. Hatched spiderlings then race up their mother's legs to her back. The babies may remain there for as little as a week or as long as a month. No one is sure what signal tells them they are ready to live on their own. When the moment comes, they all run down their mother's hairy legs at once and race away.

If spiders vanished from the earth, we would soon miss them. On summer mornings we would see no graceful webs suspended in the grass or spread in silvery mats on the ground. Insects, especially flies, would overwhelm us. If there were no spiders to spin snares or to stalk and chase down prey, human beings would have to move to another planet—leaving this one for insects to rule.

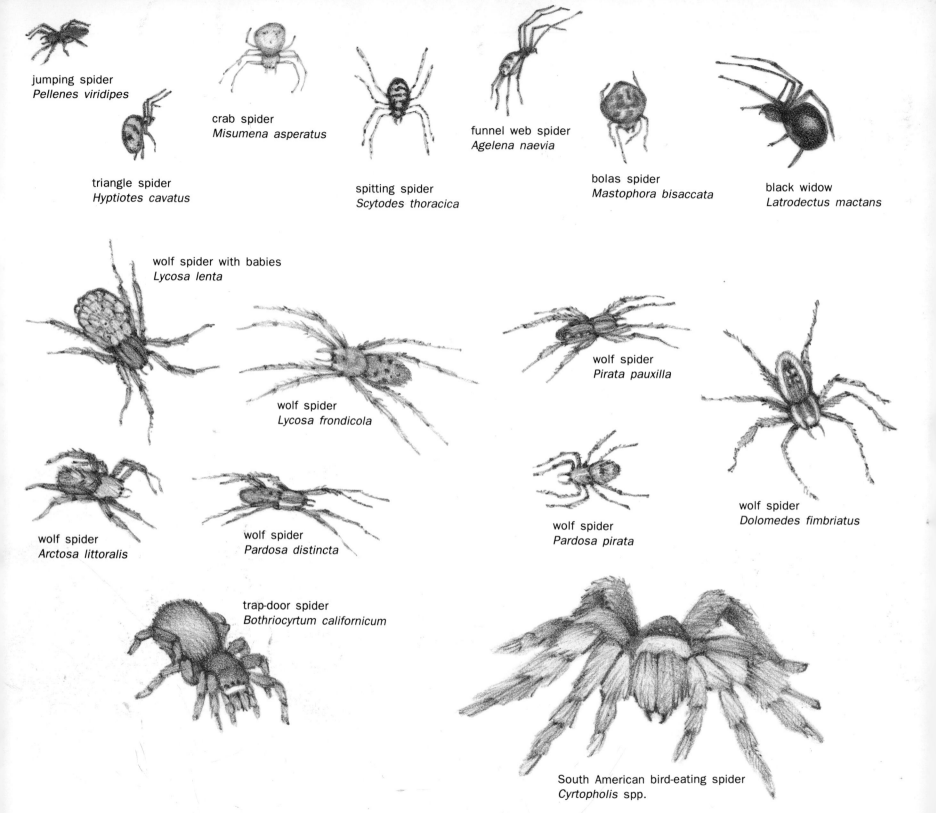

jumping spider
Pellenes viridipes

crab spider
Misumena asperatus

triangle spider
Hyptiotes cavatus

spitting spider
Scytodes thoracica

funnel web spider
Agelena naevia

bolas spider
Mastophora bisaccata

black widow
Latrodectus mactans

wolf spider with babies
Lycosa lenta

wolf spider
Lycosa frondicola

wolf spider
Pirata pauxilla

wolf spider
Arctosa littoralis

wolf spider
Pardosa distincta

wolf spider
Pardosa pirata

wolf spider
Dolomedes fimbriatus

trap-door spider
Bothriocyrtum californicum

South American bird-eating spider
Cyrtopholis spp.

The spiders on these two pages are drawn life-size. When you observe spiders, do so with respect. Don't poke them, touch them, or try to catch them. Leave spiders in peace. They are your neighbors on this planet.

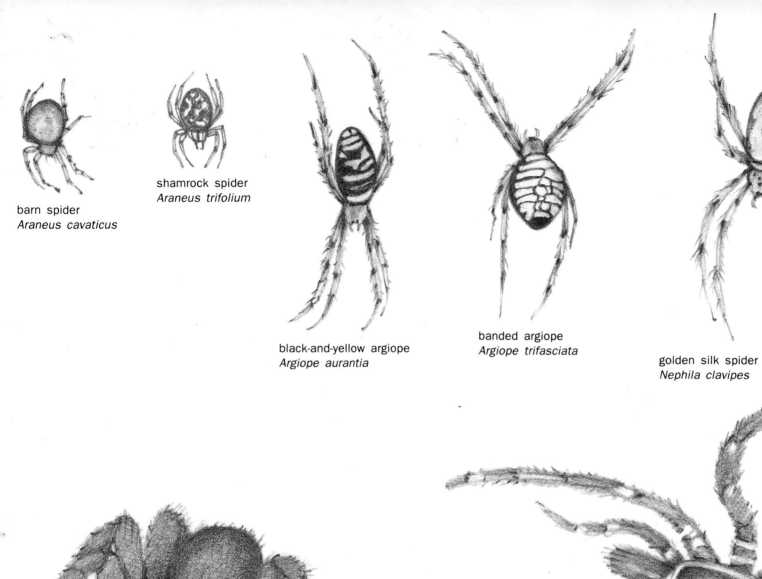

barn spider
Araneus cavaticus

shamrock spider
Araneus trifolium

black-and-yellow argiope
Argiope aurantia

banded argiope
Argiope trifasciata

golden silk spider
Nephila clavipes

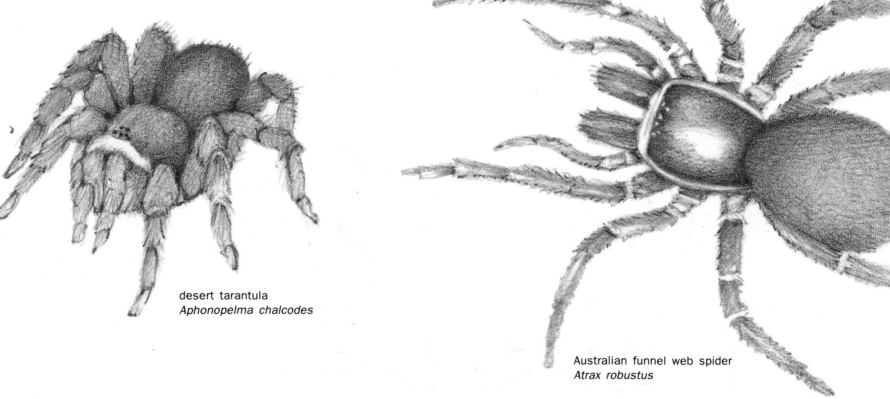

desert tarantula
Aphonopelma chalcodes

Australian funnel web spider
Atrax robustus

Index